GREEK
MYTHOLOGY

CENTAUR

BY SAMANTHA S. BELL

CONTENT CONSULTANT
ALISON C. TRAWEEK, PhD
ADJUNCT INSTRUCTOR OF GREEK AND ROMAN CLASSICS
TEMPLE UNIVERSITY

Kids Core

An Imprint of Abdo Publishing
abdobooks.com

abdobooks.com

Published by Abdo Publishing, a division of ABDO, PO Box 398166, Minneapolis, Minnesota 55439. Copyright © 2022 by Abdo Consulting Group, Inc. International copyrights reserved in all countries. No part of this book may be reproduced in any form without written permission from the publisher. Kids Core™ is a trademark and logo of Abdo Publishing.

Printed in the United States of America, North Mankato, Minnesota.
102021
012022

THIS BOOK CONTAINS
RECYCLED MATERIALS

Cover Photo: Shutterstock Images
Interior Photos: DEA/A. Dagli Orti/De Agostini/Getty Images, 4–5, 28 (top); Hoika Mikhail/Shutterstock Images, 6; Fine Art Images/Heritage Images/Hulton Fire Art Collection/Getty Images, 7, 28 (bottom); Viacheslav Lopatin/Shutterstock Images, 8; Massimo Todaro/Shutterstock Images, 10; Ruddy Gold/agefotostock/Alamy, 11; Red Line Editorial, 12; Shutterstock Images, 14–15, 16, 24, 26, 29 (top); Prisma Archivo/Alamy, 18, 29 (bottom); Frederic Soreau/agefotostock/Alamy, 20–21; DEA Picture Library/De Agostini/Getty Images, 22; Kostas Pavlis/iStockphoto, 25

Editor: Alyssa Sorenson
Series Designer: Ryan Gale

Library of Congress Control Number: 2021941516

Publisher's Cataloging-in-Publication Data

Names: Bell, Samantha S., author.
Title: Centaur / by Samantha S. Bell
Description: Minneapolis, Minnesota : Abdo Publishing, 2022 | Series: Greek mythology | Includes online resources and index.
Identifiers: ISBN 9781532196768 (lib. bdg.) | ISBN 9781098218577 (ebook)
Subjects: LCSH: Centaurs--Juvenile literature. | Animals, Mythical--Juvenile literature. | Mythology, Greek--Juvenile literature. | Gods, Greek--Juvenile literature.
Classification: DDC 292--dc23

CONTENTS

Chiron was not like other centaurs. He was peaceful instead of wild.

CHAPTER 1

THE NOBLE CENTAUR

Some ancient Greek stories talk about centaurs. These creatures are part human and part horse. Chiron was a well-known centaur. He had a man's head, arms, and **torso**. He had a horse's body and legs.

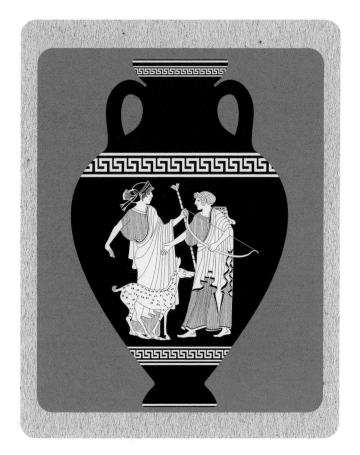

Apollo, *right*, was the god of archery. Artemis, *left*, was the goddess of wild animals and the hunt.

When Chiron was young, the god Apollo and the goddess Artemis decided to teach him. Chiron learned about medicine and music. He was also a skilled hunter. In artwork, he is often seen with a branch over his shoulder. He used the branch to carry hunted animals. Chiron was known for his wisdom.

Some artwork shows Chiron teaching Achilles how to use a bow.

Chiron later became the **tutor** of some Greek heroes. One hero was a great warrior named Achilles. Chiron taught him about medicine. The centaur also instructed the heroes Jason and Heracles.

Although the ancient Greeks lived a long time ago, people today can still see remains of their buildings.

However, Chiron was an unusual centaur. He was kind and helpful. In most stories, the centaurs were rowdy and violent. They often fought with humans.

The Centaurs in Myths

Ancient Greece existed more than 2,000 years ago. It was a civilization in southeastern Europe. The Greeks told many stories. Some were about gods, goddesses, and heroes. Other stories were about mythical creatures such as centaurs.

An Original Idea?

The idea of centaurs may not have come from Greek culture. Instead, the Greeks may have learned about centaurs through people they met while trading. For example, the Hittites were from the Middle East. They used centaur-like creatures in their art. Another theory is that centaurs were actually human invaders on horseback. They may also have been men from Thessaly, a region of Greece, hunting on horses.

Works of art, such as statues, often show centaurs as part horse.

All these stories are called myths. Greek myths often changed over time.

The description of the centaurs changed too. For instance, Homer did not say they looked like part horse. Homer was a poet. He likely lived between 800 and 700 BCE. He called centaurs "hairy beast men." Pindar was a poet who lived in the 400s BCE. He was the first one to describe centaurs as part horse.

Centaurs often used rocks or tree branches
as weapons.

Home of the Centaurs in Ancient Greece

MACEDONIA

AEGEAN SEA

EPIRUS

THESSALY

ATHENS

PELOPONNESE

ANCIENT GREECE ■
CITY ●

Ancient Greece's borders changed over time. Thessaly is one region in Greece. In Greek myths, this is where the centaurs lived.

According to the myths, many centaurs lived in a region in ancient Greece known as Thessaly. It had mountains and rivers. But mostly it had large **plains**. The Greeks used the plains for farming and raising horses. In stories, the centaurs lived in the forests of Thessaly, away from human rules and laws.

Further Evidence

Look at the website below. Does it give any new evidence to support Chapter One?

What Is Greek Mythology?

abdocorelibrary.com/centaur

Centaurs had trouble controlling their emotions. That's why they often got into fights.

CHAPTER 2

READY FOR A FIGHT

Some stories have different ideas about where centaurs came from. In one story, a king named Ixion and a cloud **nymph** had a son. They named him Centaurus. Another legend said Centaurus was the son of Apollo and a river nymph.

Heracles was a strong, powerful hero. He was the son of the Greek god Zeus.

In both stories, Centaurus became the father of the centaurs.

One well-known centaur was Pholus. One day, the hero Heracles was hunting a boar.

Pholus offered Heracles some food. He gave the hero a place to rest in his cave. Soon other centaurs joined them. After a while, they became rowdy. They attacked Heracles. The centaurs were no match for the hero, and he defeated them. Pholus and the centaur Chiron were not fighting. But they both got hurt anyway.

Living in the Stars

Like the gods, Chiron could live forever. But during the centaurs' fight with Heracles, he was struck with a poison arrow. After that, he was always in pain. Zeus was the king of the gods. To help, he moved Chiron to a place in the sky. Chiron became the **constellation** Centaurus.

Painters have shown the epic battle between the
humans and centaurs at the wedding.

An Epic Battle

In stories, centaurs often fought with humans. One story talks about the wedding of Pirithous, the Lapith king. He was going to marry a woman named Hippodamia. The centaurs were invited to the wedding. But one of the centaurs wanted the bride to leave with him. People at the wedding were not happy about that. The Lapiths fought the centaurs. The humans were victorious. They drove the centaurs away.

Explore Online

Visit the website below. Does it give any new information about Greek heroes that wasn't in Chapter Two?

Five Terrifying Tales from Greek Mythology

abdocorelibrary.com/centaur

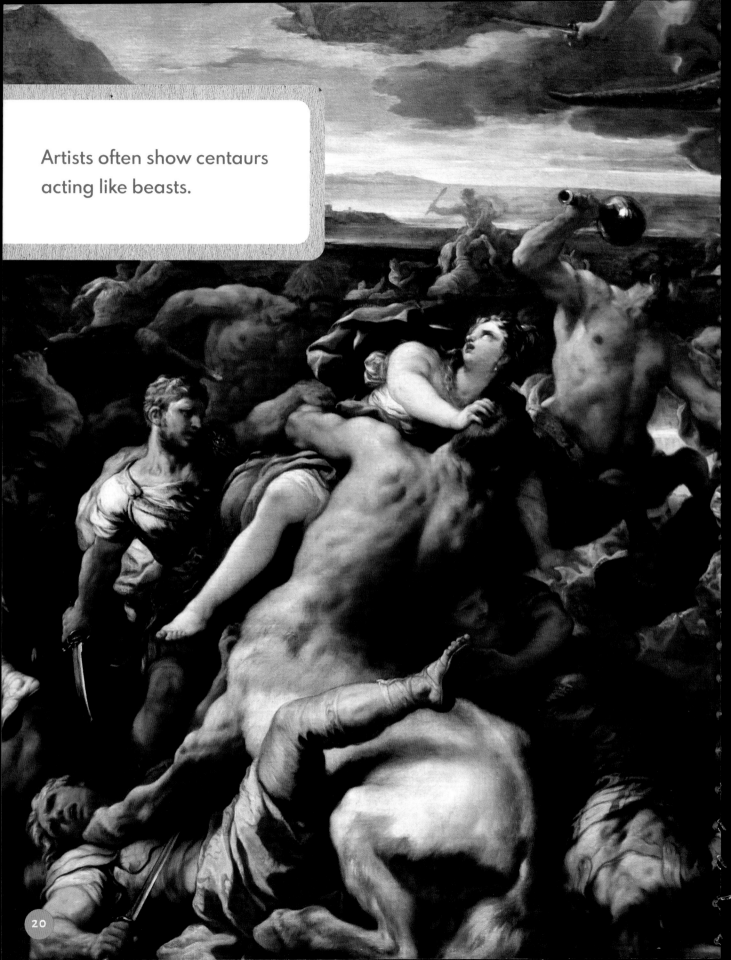

Artists often show centaurs acting like beasts.

CHAPTER 3

STORIES THROUGH ART

Ancient Greeks often used images of centaurs in their art. They are easy to recognize because of their half-human and half-horse form. The Greeks made sculptures of centaurs during the Geometric Period. This was around 900 to 700 BCE.

When archaeologists found the centaur statue from Lefkandi, its head was broken off. They carefully put the statue back together.

However, in 1969 **archaeologists** found a centaur statue at a site called Lefkandi. This centaur was even older. It was made around 900 to 1000 BCE. The centaur has a mark on its leg. The mark may represent a wound. Some people think it may be a statue of Chiron. That would mean his story has been around longer than people first thought.

The Greeks also painted centaurs on vases. Some of these feature both Chiron and Achilles. Sometimes Chiron was painted with a man's legs and wearing clothes. He still had the body and back legs of a horse though.

Female Centaurs

Not all half-human and half-horse creatures were male. Some art shows female centaurs. They are called Centaurides. But these creatures are rarely mentioned in myths.

Zeus's temple in Olympia used to be a magnificent building. The years have turned it into ruins.

Teaching Lessons

The battles between the centaurs and gods or heroes were another popular subject in Greek art. Sculptures of the battles were used to decorate buildings, especially **temples**. For example, the Temple of Zeus at Olympia, Greece, shows the battle between the centaurs and the Lapiths. A similar sculpture can be found on the Parthenon. That's a temple for the goddess Athena. It's in Athens, Greece.

Sculptures and other art help people figure out
what stories were important to the ancient Greeks.

Stories about centaurs continue to fascinate people.

Some people think myths about the centaurs may have been used to teach lessons. The centaurs were often mean and wild. When they fought the heroes, they usually lost. Their stories may have been warnings about what happens when people lose their self-control. These myths were passed down from generation to generation. People can still learn about the centaurs' stories today.

The Lefkandi statue may represent the centaur Chiron. But one archaeologist explains why that may not be the case:

> We can claim that the figure was a centaur . . . but it is not safe to assume that it had the same meaning and symbolism as in the 6th century BCE.

Source: Antonis Chaliakopoulos. "Where Did the Centaurs Come From? A Journey through Ancient Art." *Collector*, 18 Mar. 2021, thecollector.com. Accessed 7 June 2021.

What's the Big Idea?

Read this quote carefully. What is its main idea? Explain how the main idea is supported by what you learned about Greek myths.

LEGENDARY FACTS

The centaurs were creatures in Greek mythology. They were half human and half horse.

The centaur Chiron was a skilled teacher, hunter, and healer.

Centaurs were often
wild and violent.

In one story, the
Lapiths defeated
the centaurs in a
great battle.

Glossary

archaeologist
a scientist who studies human history through historical artifacts and other remains

constellation
a group of stars that form a pattern

nymph
a divine female who lives for a long time and is connected to nature

plains
large, flat lands that have few trees

temple
a building used for worship

torso
a part of the human body that extends from the neck to the hips

tutor
a private teacher

Online Resources

To learn more about centaurs, visit our free resource websites below.

Visit **abdocorelibrary.com** or scan this QR code for free Common Core resources for teachers and students, including vetted activities, multimedia, and booklinks, for deeper subject comprehension.

Visit **abdobooklinks.com** or scan this QR code for free additional online weblinks for further learning. These links are routinely monitored and updated to provide the most current information available.

Learn More

Hudak, Heather C. *Artemis*. Abdo, 2022.

Marcus, Richard. *Introduction to Greek Mythology for Kids*. Ulysses, 2021.

Menzies, Jean. *Greek Myths*. DK, 2020.

Index

About the Author

Samantha S. Bell lives in the foothills of the Blue Ridge Mountains. She has written more than 100 nonfiction books for kids on topics ranging from penguins to tractors to surviving on a deserted island.